This book belongs to

....

How this collection works

This collection of traditional tales offers four well-loved stories from around the world for you and your child to enjoy together: *The King and his Wish, Rabbit on the Run, Boxer and the Fish* and *Cook, Pot, Cook!* They are based on traditional stories that your child may already be familiar with, but have been written so that your child can read them for themselves. They are carefully levelled and in line with your child's phonics learning at school. In addition, each story is accompanied by an optional extended story text for parents to read aloud to their child, to offer the richness that the original story language provides.

How to use this book

Find a time to read with your child when they are happy to concentrate for about 5–10 minutes. Reading with your child should be a shared and enjoyable experience. Choose one or two stories for each session, so they don't get too tired.

Please read the tips on the next page of this collection, as they offer suggestions and ideas for how to get the most out of this story collection.

Enjoy sharing the stories!

Tips for reading the stories together

Step 1 – Before you begin, ask your child to read the title of the story. Talk about what the story might be about. To set the scene of the story, read the extended story text available before each story. This will provide the rich story language of the original story and will familiarise the child with the plot and the characters before they read the story for themselves. Talk about the story and what your child liked and didn't like.

Step 2 – Now encourage your child to read the illustrated story to you. Talk about the pictures as you read. Your child will be able to read most of the words in the story, but if they struggle with a word, remind them to say the sounds in the word from left to right and then blend the sounds together to read the whole word, e.g. w-i-sh, wish. If they come across a tricky word that they cannot sound out, simply read the word to the child, e.g. was, you, me.

Step 3 – After you have read the story, talk about what happened. How are all the different characters feeling at the end of the story? Encourage your child to use the story map that follows each story to retell the story to you in their own words. It's a fun way of helping them to understand the story and to learn to tell stories in their own way.

Contents

OXFORD
UNIVERSITY PRESS

The King and his Wish

Once in a far off land, there lived a king who wanted to touch the moon. So he climbed to the top of a very tall hill.

The King stretched and he stre-e-e-tched! But he couldn't touch the moon.

"Bring me a box to stand on!" he ordered. "I wish to touch the moon."

So his servants went to the palace and found an enormous, red box and carried it up the hill to the King.

The King climbed onto the red box. He stood on the tips of his toes. He stretched and stre-e-e-tched! But he couldn't touch the moon.

"Bring me another box!" he ordered. "I wish to touch the moon."

So the servants ran to fetch another box.

The King looked up at the moon. He saw that the moon was a very long way off. "I'm going to need lots more boxes!" he shouted. So the servants searched throughout the land, until every box was found and brought to the King.

The servants made a tower out of the boxes and the King climbed to the top. He stretched and stre-e-e-tched! But *still* he couldn't touch the moon.

"Bring me another box!" he ordered. "I wish to touch the moon."

So the servants passed up another box. He stood on the tips of his toes. He stretched and stre-e-e-tched! But *still* the King couldn't touch the moon.

"I need more boxes!" he shouted. So the servants passed the King the *very last* box.

The King climbed onto the very last box. He stood on the tips of his toes. He stretched and stre-e-e-tched! But still the King couldn't *quite* touch the moon.

"If only I had *one more* box," he thought, "then I could touch the moon."

"Pass me the big red box from the bottom of the tower," he ordered.

"No! No!" cried the servants. "We cannot do that! You will fall!"

"But I am the King," shouted the King. "You must do as I wish!" And he stamped his foot hard and shouted, "You will pass me the big red box, NOW!"

"As you wish!" said his servants.

But as they pulled the big red box from the bottom of the tower, the tower began to wobble …

Then CRASH! BANG! WALLOP! Down fell the tower of boxes. And down fell the King. Luckily, the King was not hurt. But everyone laughed at him for being so silly!

The King and his Wish

Written by Alison Hawes

Illustrated by Kate Slater

The King had a wish.

I wish to go up!

8

9

The King got a big, red box.

11

14

But I am the King! **You will get me that red box!**

18

19

And he fell with a ...

Retell the story

Once upon a time...

The end.

Rabbit on the Run

Once upon a time, there was a rabbit. Rabbit thought he was the best runner in the world. He was very boastful about his running.

"You cannot get me!" he shouted to his friends.

One day, Rabbit decided to see how fast he could run. He set off, with his ears flying behind him in the breeze.

"I'm so fast!" he boasted.

Then Tortoise came along. Tortoise was big and slow, but he wanted to race with Rabbit.

"I can get you, Rabbit!" called out Tortoise.

"Who's that calling?" thought Rabbit. "It can't be Tortoise!"

"Do you really want to race me?" said Rabbit.

"Yes, I do!" said Tortoise.

"All right then – let's race!" shouted Rabbit.

Rabbit got into the lead very quickly. He could not resist turning round to boast to Tortoise, "You cannot get me!"

"We shall see, Rabbit," said Tortoise.

Rabbit ran and ran, until he could not see Tortoise anymore.

"You cannot get me!" Rabbit shouted. Tortoise carried on, slowly and steadily.

"We shall see, Rabbit," he said.

Rabbit ran and ran. But then he started to slow down. "Oooh, I am very tired," he said. "I'll just have a little rest. Tortoise will never catch up." And he sat down under a tree, and had a nap.

Tortoise, meanwhile, had been carrying on, slowly and steadily. Then he saw Rabbit – asleep! "Shhh!" whispered Tortoise, and he walked carefully past Rabbit.

Suddenly, Rabbit woke up. "What's happened?" he said. "Where's Tortoise? I've slept too long!"

Rabbit could see Tortoise up ahead. He still thought he could beat him.

"You cannot get me, I'm still going to win!" he shouted to Tortoise.

"We shall see, Rabbit," said Tortoise.

Tortoise was nearly at the finishing line! Rabbit ran and ran, but there was too much ground to make up. Tortoise calmly walked over the finishing line – just in front of the racing Rabbit.

Tortoise came first, and Rabbit came second. Rabbit was very sad.

"I did not get you," he said.

"Never mind, Rabbit," said Tortoise. "You tried hard, and that's what counts."

Rabbit on the Run

Written by Alex Lane

Illustrated by Laura Hughes

Rabbit was quick.

Rabbit was on the run.

Hang on!

29

Rabbit shot off.

Rabbit ran and ran.

You cannot get me!

33

Rabbit had a nap.

Rabbit got up.

Rabbit was in a rush.

Once upon a time...

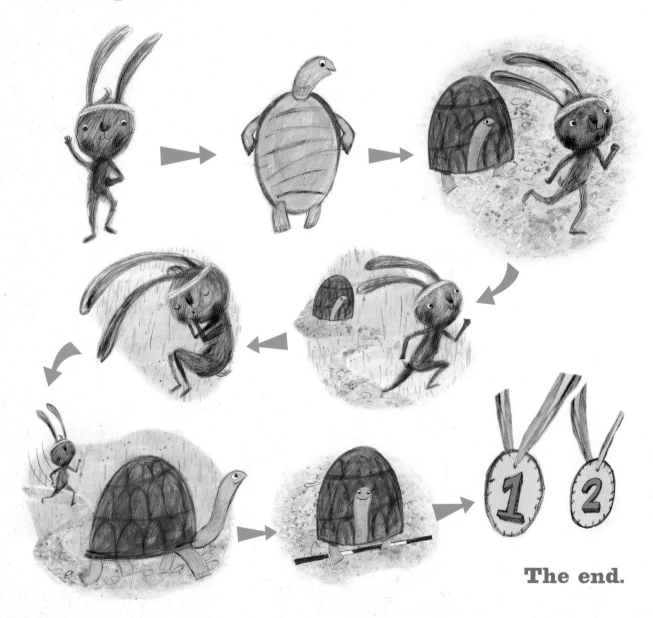

The end.

40

Boxer and the Fish `Extended Story`

Once upon a time, there was a dog called Boxer. Now, Boxer had one big weakness. He was just too fond of food. In fact, you could say he was really rather greedy!

One day, Boxer decided to go into town to look for food. As he neared the town, he began to get excited and started to run. He didn't even glance at the stall selling delicious fruit because he had spotted something ahead that looked more interesting. Can you guess what it was?

It was a fish shop! Boxer peeped round the door and looked around him.

The shop was full of every kind of fish, but the one that caught Boxer's eye was the biggest fish he had ever seen. Boxer's mouth began to water as he thought about the fish. Can you guess what he did?

Boxer leapt onto the counter, grabbed the enormous fish and ran off with it as fast as he could. The fishmonger was very angry and ran out of the shop shouting, "Stop!".

Boxer was too quick for the fishmonger and had soon left the shop far behind. As he ran off down the road he passed two cats. They envied Boxer, they would have enjoyed a fish just like that for their dinner.

Boxer wanted to find somewhere quiet to eat his enormous fish in peace, so when he saw the entrance to the park he ran in.

Boxer found his way to the quietest part of the park where there was a deep pool.

As he neared the pool, something in the water caught Boxer's eye. He stood still and looked into the water. Can you guess what he saw?

Boxer saw another dog looking up at him. It had a fish in its mouth just like he did.

"Wait a minute," thought Boxer, "I have got an enormous fish but that dog has a **gigantic** fish."

Well, this was when Boxer's greed got the better of him. Boxer decided that the other dog's fish was bigger than his and he wanted it. He opened his mouth ready to bark. What do you think happened?

As Boxer opened his mouth to bark, his enormous fish fell into the pool! At that moment Boxer realised his mistake, but it was too late. The fish was gone forever. He looked into the pool and saw that the other dog had lost its fish too.

Boxer wandered back home feeling very sorry for himself. He lay down in front of his kennel and was very sad. There would be no fish for Boxer tonight. But that was that.

Boxer and the Fish

Written by Monica Hughes

Illustrated by Ann Ruozhu Sun

Boxer was a big dog.

Boxer ran into town to look for food.

In a shop was ...

47

He ran down the road.

Boxer ran into the park.

In the park was a deep pool.

Boxer took a good look.
In the deep pool was ...

... a dog!

The fish fell in the pool.

No! My fish!

Boxer was sad.

No dinner for me!

Retell the story

Once upon a time...

The end.

Cook, Pot, Cook!

There was once a little girl who lived with her mum and her nan. One day there was no food left in their house. The little girl thought, "I know what to do!" So she went into the kitchen and took the biggest pot she could find down from the shelf.

She put the pot on the kitchen table and said the magic words, "Cook, pot, cook!" Straightaway, the pot began to fill with sweet, hot porridge.

"Quick, Mum! Look at this!" said the girl. Mum couldn't believe her eyes! The pot was filling up with sweet, hot porridge.

"This is a magic cooking pot!" Mum said.

"Quick, Nan! Look at this!" said the girl.

Nan couldn't believe her eyes! The pot was now full of sweet, hot porridge. "We can have porridge for breakfast!" she said.

When the pot was full, the little girl said, "Stop, pot, stop!" And the pot stopped cooking. But Mum and Nan were so busy eating they didn't hear the magic words.

That night, Nan was feeling hungry again. But there was still no food in the house. So she went into the kitchen and took the biggest pot she could find down from the shelf.

She put the pot on the kitchen table and said the magic words, "Cook, pot, cook!" Straightaway, the pot began to fill with sweet, hot porridge. Soon Nan had eaten a big bowl of sweet, hot porridge.

But even though Nan had finished her supper, the pot wouldn't stop making porridge. Soon the magic pot was full and the porridge dripped onto the floor. Nan didn't know what to do. So she climbed onto a chair to get out of the way of the porridge.

Mum saw the porridge run like a river out of the door taking Nan with it. She ran after Nan and the magic pot, but she couldn't stop the pot making porridge.

The little girl saw the porridge run like a river down the road taking Nan with it. But luckily she knew what to do.

"Stop, pot, stop!" she shouted and straightaway the magic pot stopped cooking.

But by now, the whole town was covered in sweet, hot porridge. Luckily, the townspeople didn't seem to mind. They had all the sweet, hot porridge they could eat for their supper! After that, Nan always remembered to say, "Stop, pot, stop!" when she used the magic cooking pot!

Cook, Pot, Cook!

Written by David Bedford

Illustrated by Jimothy Rolovio

Tess got a pot.

The pot was boiling.

Look at all the food, Mum!

That night ...

Yum-yum!

68

The pot was full! It did not stop!

Look at all the food, Mum!

71

The food got to Nan in her chair.

Look at all the food, Nan!

Once upon a time...

The end.

Make up a new story!

Now have a go at making up your own story like the ones in this book. You can use the ideas here or make up your own!

1 Who is in your story?

2 What happens first?

Perhaps Rabbit tries to help the King reach the moon?

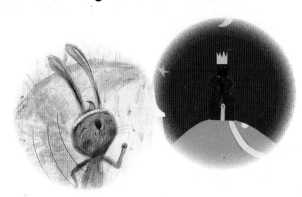

Perhaps Tess tries to magic up some food for Boxer?

3 What happens then?

Does Rabbit help the King stop wanting the moon?

Does Tess get a yummy fish for Boxer?

4 How will your story end?

Will the King give the rabbit a reward?

Will Tess and Boxer eat the fish for tea?

OXFORD
UNIVERSITY PRESS

Great Clarendon Street, Oxford, OX2 6DP, United Kingdom

Oxford University Press is a department of the University
of Oxford. It furthers the University's objective of excellence
in research, scholarship, and education by publishing worldwide.
Oxford is a registered trade mark of Oxford University Press
in the UK and in certain other countries

Text © Oxford University Press 2011

The King and his Wish Illustrations © Kate Slater 2011
Rabbit on the Run Illustrations © Laura Hughes 2011
Boxer and the Fish Illustrations © Ann Ruozhu Sun 2011
Cook, Pot, Cook! Illustrations © Jimothy Rolovio 2011

Extended story text for *The King and his Wish* written by Alison Hawes
Extended story text for *Rabbit on the Run* written by Teresa Heapy
Extended story text for *Boxer and the Fish* written by Monica Hughes
Extended story text for *Cook, Pot, Cook!* written by Alison Hawes

The moral rights of the author have been asserted

The King and his Wish, Rabbit on the Run, Boxer and the Fish,
Cook, Pot, Cook! first published 2011
This edition published 2018

British Library Cataloguing in Publication Data
Data available

ISBN: 978-0-19-276516-1

10 9 8 7 6 5 4 3 2 1

Paper used in the production of this book is a natural, recyclable
product made from wood grown in sustainable forests. The
manufacturing process conforms to the environmental
regulations of the country of origin.

Printed in China

Acknowledgements

Series Advisor: Nikki Gamble